THE ROMANS

HISTORY PROJECT PACK WITH LOTS OF USEFUL FACTS AND FUN ACTIVITIES

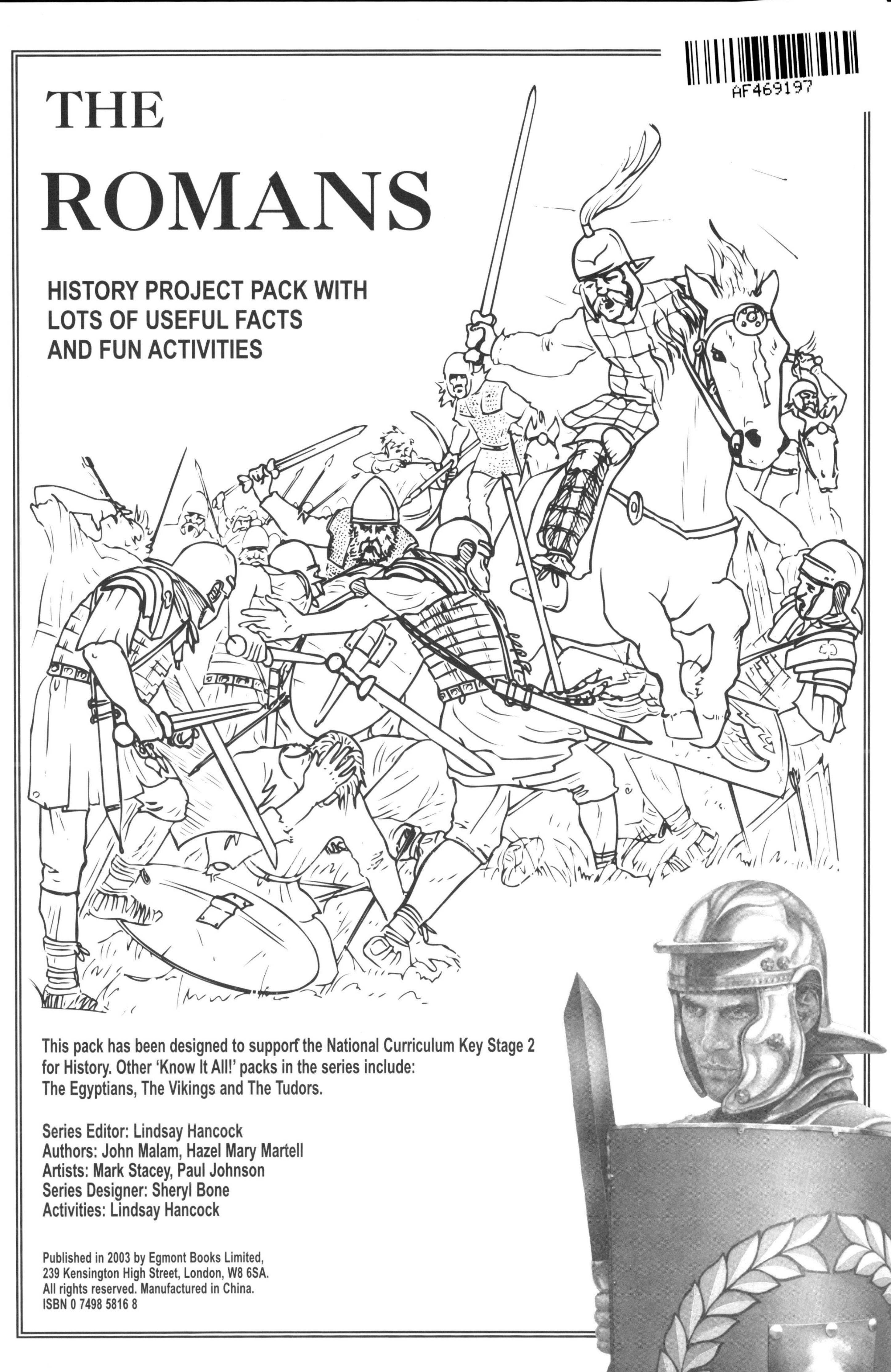

This pack has been designed to support the National Curriculum Key Stage 2 for History. Other 'Know It All!' packs in the series include: The Egyptians, The Vikings and The Tudors.

Series Editor: Lindsay Hancock
Authors: John Malam, Hazel Mary Martell
Artists: Mark Stacey, Paul Johnson
Series Designer: Sheryl Bone
Activities: Lindsay Hancock

Published in 2003 by Egmont Books Limited,
239 Kensington High Street, London, W8 6SA.

Manufactured in China.
ISBN 0 7498 5816 8

WELCOME TO THE ROMANS

CONTENTS:

WHO WERE THE ROMANS?

Where did the Romans come from?

The Romans came from the country we now call **Italy**. At the start of the 8th century BC, many different tribes of people lived there. Two of the tribes were the **Etruscans** and the **Latins**, both of whom built villages and towns. One of the towns was Rome, built on the banks of the River Tiber. The people who lived there were mostly Latins. As Rome grew in size, its people became known as Romans, but their language was still called Latin.

NORTH
RIVER TIBER
ETRUSCANS
ROME
LATINS
ITALY
TYRRHENIAN SEA
SICILY

When did the Romans live?

At first, Rome was just a small settlement, but it slowly grew larger, richer and more powerful. Towards the end of the 3rd century BC, the Romans began to conquer neighbouring lands and build up a large empire. The Roman empire reached its greatest extent about 400 years later, in the 2nd century AD.

How was Rome founded?

Legend says that Rome was founded by a man called **Romulus**. He had a twin brother called **Remus**. Just after the twins were born, their great uncle threw them into the River Tiber, hoping they would drown. But they were rescued by a she-wolf and brought up by a shepherd. When they became young men they were reunited with their grandfather, King Numitor. The twins founded the city of Rome, but they could not decide which of them should be the ruler. They fought over who should rule Rome. In the fight, Remus was killed, leaving Romulus to become the first ruler. According to legend, Rome was founded in 753BC.

DO YOU KNOW YOUR ROMAN NUMERALS?

I	= 1	VI	= 6	XX	= 20	LXX	= 70
II	= 2	VII	= 7	XXX	= 30	LXXX	= 80
III	= 3	VIII	= 8	XL	= 40	XC	= 90
IV	= 4	IX	= 9	L	= 50	C	= 100
V	= 5	X	= 10	LX	= 60	D	= 500

E.g. 13 XIII (10 + 3)

25 XXV (10 + 10 + 5)

93 XCIII (90 + 3)

Complete these sentences with Roman numerals.

I am ________ years old.

My house number is ________.

I have ________ pairs of shoes.

I go to school ________ days a week.

Today's date is ________ of ______________ (write the month).

My birthday is on ________ of ____________ (write the month).

ROMAN EMPERORS

3

Who was the first Roman Emperor? ▶

The first Roman emperor was **Octavian**. He was the nephew of Julius Caesar, the famous soldier. When Octavian became emperor in 27BC, he was given a new name. From then on he was called **Augustus**, which means Great. Augustus ruled until AD14 and brought a time of peace to Rome and its empire.

◀ **Nero** was emperor from AD54 to AD68. He was famous for his cruelty. He murdered one wife to marry another one, and then killed her too. In AD68 he was forced to flee from Rome as people revolted against him.

Trajan was emperor ▶ from AD99 to AD117. He was a successful soldier who conquered Dacia (now Romania) and added it to the empire. He also reduced the taxes people had to pay and had many public buildings erected.

Constantine ▶ ruled from AD306 to AD337. He was the first emperor to become a Christian. He made changes to the army and to the way the empire was run. He founded the city of **Constantinople** (now known as Istanbul), in Turkey.

◀ **Hadrian** became emperor in AD117. He toured the provinces (countries) which made up the Roman empire. He made sure they were well defended. He came to Britain and ordered a defensive wall to be built in the north of the country. We call this wall **Hadrian's Wall**.

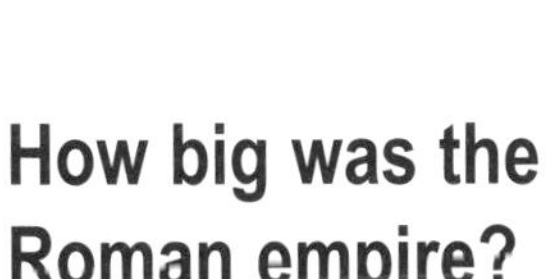

How big was the Roman empire?

At its largest, the Roman empire stretched from Britain and Portugal in the west to Asia Minor (Turkey) in the east. It also included all the lands around the Mediterranean and the whole of Egypt.

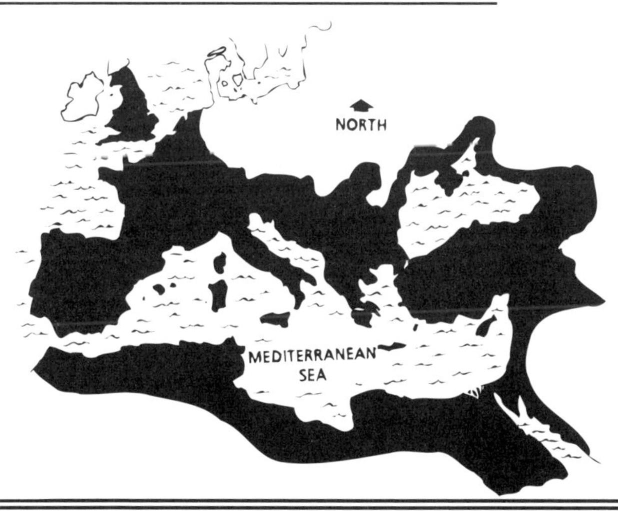

JULIUS CAESAR

What was Julius Caesar like?

Julius Caesar was born into a wealthy Roman family around 100BC. He was a brilliant soldier, a shrewd politician and a skilful author, who wrote detailed accounts of his campaigns. He was also ambitious and vain and hid his bald head under a wig!

Did he conquer any countries?

Around 60BC Caesar became the governor of northern Italy. While he was there, he realised he could gain the wealth and glory he wanted if he conquered **Gaul** (France and Belgium). He started to invade Gaul in 58BC. Within three years he had conquered most of the country. Then, in 55BC and 54BC, Caesar sent expeditions across the sea to Britain. He wanted to add Britain to the Roman empire too. But he failed, and his army went back to Gaul.

Did he rule over the Romans?

While Caesar was in Gaul, a war broke out in Rome itself. Caesar saw this as a chance to become even more important. He marched back to Rome with his army. In 48BC he defeated an army lead by Pompey, one of Rome's most important men. Two years later, Caesar was given the title 'Father of his Country'.

In 44BC, however, he said that he wanted to be called 'Dictator for Life'. By calling himself Dictator, Caesar had tried to make himself the most powerful Roman alive. He wanted to rule the Roman empire just as a king would, with everyone taking orders from him. Many people were unhappy with this. They were used to being ruled by a group of men chosen in an election. The men were called **senators**.

How did Julius Caesar die?

Some of the senators thought that Julius Caesar had become too powerful. They were afraid he really would make himself into a king. To stop this from happening, a group of senators plotted against him. In 44BC Caesar was stabbed to death.

ROME - CAPITAL OF AN EMPIRE

5

How did Rome start?

In the 8th century BC, Rome was a collection of small farming villages built on seven hills on the banks of the River Tiber. Its wealth came from farming and from trade. By about 750BC it began to grow into a city when marshes near the river were drained. The land that used to be marsh was used to make a public square. At the same time, walls were built around two of the seven hills to defend the city.

How many people lived there?

Although Rome started off small, it soon began to expand. People came from all over Italy to live there. As the Roman empire grew, people from other countries moved there too. By the 1st century AD, Rome had a population of over one million people.

How was Roman society organised?

Roman society was divided into two main classes. These were the **patricians** (sounds like: pa-trish-ans) who were the wealthy ruling classes who owned a lot of land, and the **plebeians** (sounds like: pleb-ee-ans) who were tradesmen, craftworkers, servants and men with small farms. There were also vast numbers of slaves who did all the dirty, heavy or difficult work.

Was Rome ever in danger?

In the early years of its history, Rome was often in danger of being attacked by armies of **Celts** from the north. Around 390BC the Celts defeated the Romans at the Battle of Allia. They went on to attack Rome, causing great destruction. As Rome got a more powerful army, such attacks became impossible. In AD64, however, much of the city was destroyed in a great fire and had to be rebuilt.

BUILDINGS OF ROME

6

The Colosseum was a huge amphitheatre. It was four storeys high, 188m long and 156m wide. It could seat 47,000 people who watched spectacular entertainments such as fights between gladiators and wild animals. The arena could also be flooded for mock naval battles.

The Forum was much bigger and grander than any other forum in the empire. It was a huge, paved area in the heart of the city surrounded by important public buildings, temples of the gods Jupiter, Saturn and Venus, as well as temples to the emperors who the Romans believed had become gods when they died. The forum was also the market place, with shops around the sides and stalls in the middle on market days.

The Pantheon was a circular temple where many different gods were worshipped. Other cities had them, but the one in Rome was the most famous. It was built from concrete – a building material which the Romans were experts at using. Buildings made from concrete could be put up quickly, and shapes such as domes and arches could be made. The dome of its roof was 43m wide.

The Circus Maximus was where people went to watch chariot racing. It was the biggest race track in the Roman empire. It could hold an audience of 100,000 people. It was gradually made bigger until it could hold 350,000 people.

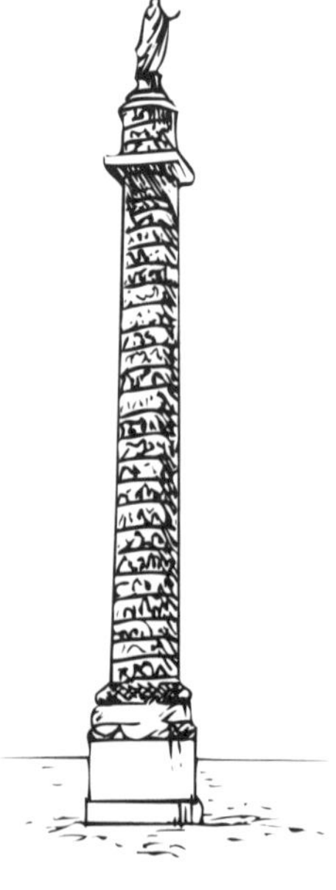

Trajan's Column is the most famous of the many columns and statues which were erected in the Forum in Rome. It stands 38m high and is decorated with carvings, showing scenes from Trajan's military victories in Dacia (Romania).

ROMANS IN BRITAIN

When did the Romans come to Britain?

Julius Caesar had tried to conquer Britain in 55BC and 54BC. He was unsuccessful and the Romans did not come back again until AD43. This time, about 40,000 soldiers sailed from Gaul to Kent and defeated the British armies in a two-day battle at the River Medway. The emperor Claudius led them into Colchester, where 11 British kings surrendered to him.

Who lived in Britain at the time?

At the time of the Roman invasions, Britain was inhabited by people known as the Celts. They were divided into many different tribes, each with its own ruler, and were often at war with each other. They did not all want to be part of the Roman empire and there were a lot of rebellions against Roman rule. The most violent rebellion was led by **Queen Boudicca** (sounds like: boo-dik-a), the Queen of the Iceni (sounds like: eye-seen-eye). With her army she destroyed the towns of Colchester, London and St Albans before she was defeated.

Did the Romans build towns?

Once the Romans were settled in Britain, they began to build towns with streets, open squares and public buildings, as well as houses made from brick or stone. Their towns became centres of trade and many of them are still towns today. They include York, Chester, Colchester, Lincoln, London and Gloucester.

Did the Romans build roads?

Building good roads was one of the first tasks after the Romans invaded Britain. This meant they could move soldiers quickly around the country. Roman roads were carefully built. Surveyors planned the road to run as straight as possible. Engineers cleared the ground and laid foundations of clay, chalk or gravel. On top of this they put cement and paving stones so the roads could be used in wet weather as well as when it was dry. Some modern British roads still follow routes laid out by the Romans, almost 2,000 years ago.

Why did they build Hadrian's Wall?

The Romans hoped to conquer the whole of Britain, but they did not succeed. They found that the further north they went, the more people fought against them. So, in AD122 they started to build a stone wall between the River Solway and the River Tyne. It was the idea of the emperor Hadrian. It was 120km long and had 16 large forts, with smaller ones in between. Parts of it were painted white, so it could be seen easily from a distance. Hadrian's Wall was the northern boundary of the Roman empire.

Why did they leave Britain?

The Romans stayed in Britain for over 350 years. From about AD280, however, they had to defend the country against invaders who were attacking from the north and east. By the end of the 4th century AD the Roman empire began to fall apart. Rome was ruled by weak emperors who were not able to govern distant provinces. Even worse, Rome itself was attacked by barbarian tribes. Soldiers were brought from all parts of the empire to defend Rome. By AD410 the last Roman soldiers were withdrawn from Britain. When the Roman army left, the Roman age in Britain came to an end.

Did they go to Ireland?

People used to think that the Romans never went to Ireland. There was no mention of them going there in any books which were written at the time, and very few Roman objects had been found. In the 1990's, however, archaeologists started to dig up a settlement at Drumanagh, near Dublin, where they found lots of Roman objects. Some people think this is proof the Romans did go to Ireland. Others say it only shows that the local Irish people traded with the Romans.

FOOD

9

How did they eat?

Wealthy Romans did not eat their meals at tables, like we do. Instead, they lay on couches, usually propping themselves up on one elbow, and ate their food from low tables. Nine was thought to be an ideal number for dinner, with three people to a couch on three sides of the table. The fourth side was left open for the servants to carry the dishes in and out. Most food was eaten from shared dishes, with each diner using a spoon or fingers to get his or her share. Finger-bowls were also provided for washing food off fingers between courses.

What did they eat?

The first meal of the day was breakfast, which was usually bread and cheese. It was followed by lunch which was usually cold meat or fish, bread and fruit. Dinner was the main meal and it was often served around four o'clock in the afternoon. It was usually made up of three courses, each with several things to choose from.

What did they drink?

Wine was the main drink for Roman adults. They had both red and white winc. It was often watered down before serving and was sometimes flavoured with honey. Children drank milk, which was also thought to be suitable for the sick and weak.

A Roman feast

The first course might have been food such as eggs, shellfish (especially oysters), olives and lettuce.

The next course was usually meat or fish, together with vegetables such as cabbage, leeks, peas or onions, flavoured with herbs and spices such as fennel, thyme, sage, mint, coriander, pepper and ginger. Olive oil was used in a lot of recipes and the Romans were also fond of a fish sauce called 'garum', which was made from salted fish. The meat included beef, mutton, pork, chicken, wild boar, venison, game birds and hares, while the fish dishes included octopus, eel and lobster. All of these could be served boiled, grilled, fried or stewed. The very rich also sometimes ate things such as peacocks, ostriches and even dormice!

The third course of the meal was usually fruit, such as grapes, water-melons and dates. It was often eaten raw, but was sometimes cooked and sweetened with honey. Honey cakes and stuffed dates were also popular.

HONEY SPICED ROMAN CAKES

Note: This recipe contains nuts.

You will need an adult's permission and help with this recipe.

Ingredients

200g self-raising flour
$\frac{1}{2}$ tsp ground nutmeg
$\frac{1}{2}$ tsp ground cinnamon
80g ground almonds
60g sugar
1 egg (size 3/medium)
milk
runny honey
chopped nuts

Equipment

mixing bowl
wooden spoon
small bowl
greased baking tray

1. Put the flour, nutmeg, cinnamon, almonds and sugar into a mixing bowl. Stir together well.
2. Break the egg into another bowl. Add a little milk. Beat together well.
3. Add the egg mixture to the flour. Beat well. Add more milk or flour to make a firm mixture.
4. Dust your hands with a little flour. Shape the mixture into 12 small cakes. Place on a greased baking tray.
5. Bake in a pre-heated oven for 30 minutes or until golden brown (Gas mark 5, 375°F,190°C).
6. Spoon a little honey over each cake whilst still hot. Garnish with chopped nuts. Eat on day of baking.

EDUCATION

Who was educated in Roman times?

All Roman children were educated at home until they were about seven years old. They learned to be obedient, helpful and truthful.

What were schools like?

Schoolmasters set up schools in a room in their own houses or rented a room from somebody else. The pupils had seats but no desks and the books they read from were written on papyrus scrolls. They started lessons at dawn, but finished early in the afternoon.

The schoolmasters were usually very strict and were quite ready to hit their pupils with a strap or cane to make them learn or behave better.

What did children learn at school?

During the 3rd century BC, the Romans started to set up schools where children could be educated from the age of seven. These schools were open to all boys and girls whose parents could afford to pay for them to go. The lessons included reading and writing, in both Latin and Greek, and arithmetic, which was done with the help of a counting frame called an **abacus**.

Both boys and girls went to these schools until they were about eleven years old. Girls then stayed at home and learned how to manage the house and its servants, while boys went on to another school called a '**grammaticus**'. There they read the works of famous Roman and Greek writers and poets, and learned history and geometry, as well as arithmetic. Some also learned music and athletics.

Were there any colleges?

Boys left their 'grammaticus' at the age of sixteen. Many of them then took a job or joined the army. Those who wanted a career in law, politics or medicine went on to special tutors to learn more. To do this, they often had to travel to one of the Roman provinces. Athens, in Greece, was one of the favourite places.

GODS AND GODDESSES

Did the Romans have many gods?

The Romans believed in many different gods and goddesses. They thought they were all around them, rather than in one special place. They also thought that the gods and goddesses influenced everything they did. Most of the Roman gods and goddesses were the same as the ones the Greeks had worshipped before them, but most of them had different names. The exception was the god of the arts, music and light who was called **Apollo** by both the Greeks and the Romans. Some of the main gods and goddesses are shown here.

◀ Jupiter

The most important of the Roman gods. The Greeks had called him Zeus. He was the god of the sky and the king of all the other gods.

Juno ▶

The wife of Jupiter. The Greeks had called her Hera. She was the goddess of women and mothers. All the other gods belonged to Jupiter and Juno's family.

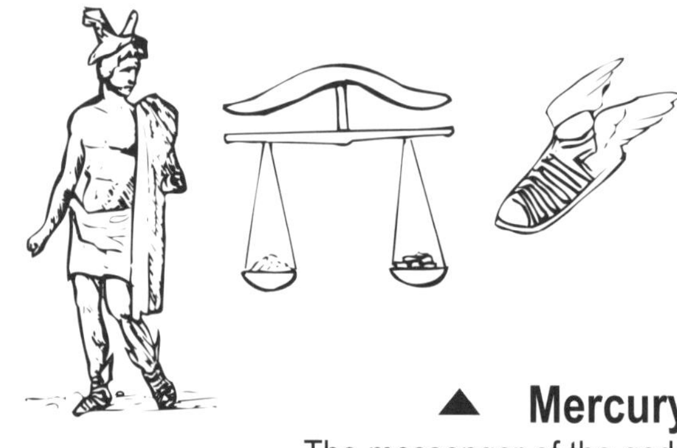

Bacchus ▶

The god of wine.

▲ Mercury

The messenger of the gods and also the god of trade.

Neptune ▶

The god of the sea and fresh water springs.

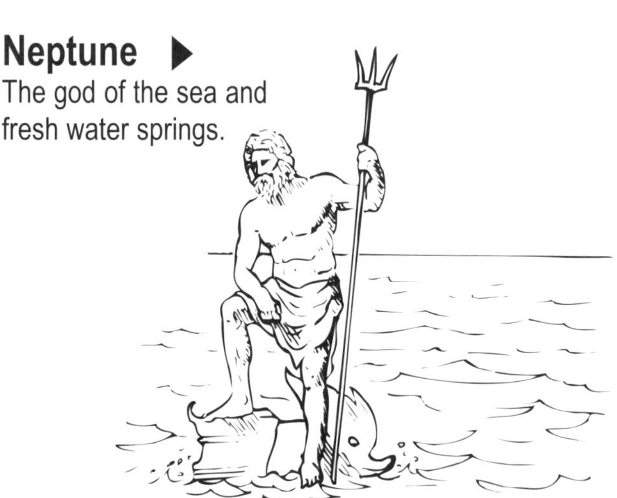

Mars ▶

The god of war.

Saturn
The god of farming.

Minerva
The goddess of crafts and wisdom.

Vulcan
The god of fire.

Venus
The goddess of beauty and love.

Diana
The goddess of the light of the moon and of hunting.

Ceres
The goddess of farming and crops.

Vesta
The goddess of the hearth.

What were Roman temples like?

The Romans built many temples to their gods and goddesses. They did not go there to pray, however. Instead they thought the temple was a home for the god or goddess. Inside there was a shrine with a statue of the god or goddess. Each temple had a number of priests or priestesses who did everything possible to please the gods.

Did they make sacrifices?

The Romans thought they had to please the gods to have their wishes granted. They thought the best way to do this was by making them gifts of food or precious objects. The priests and priestesses also sacrificed animals outside the temples on feast days.

UNSCRAMBLE THE GODS

Unscramble the letters to spell the names of the gods and goddesses.

NETUPEN

— — — — — — —

God of the sea and fresh water springs.

NIDAA

— — — — —

Goddess of the light of the moon and of hunting.

REPUJIT

— — — — — — —

God of the sky and king of all other gods.

SENUV

— — — — —

Goddess of beauty and love.

SRUNAT

— — — — — —

God of farming.

THE ROMAN ARMY

How was the army organised?

The army was divided into **legions**. A legion had about 5,500 soldiers in it. Each legion was divided into ten **cohorts**. A cohort was divided into six **centuries**. Each century had 80 soldiers in it. These were the footsoldiers who were known as **legionaries**. At the head of each century was a **centurion**. He gave commands to his men and made sure they obeyed them. As well as its footsoldiers, each legion had about 120 cavalrymen and a **standard bearer**. The standard bearer carried the legion's standard. This was a long pole with a silver eagle on top as the emblem of Rome. It was a disgrace for the standard to be lost. The standard bearer wore animal skins over his armour to make him look more fearsome in battle.

Did they wear a uniform?

Roman soldiers wore a uniform to protect themselves and to recognise each other in battle. They each wore an iron helmet, a woollen tunic under a cuirass (a tunic made from leather and plated with metal) and a kilt made of leather strips. In warm climates, they went bare-legged and wore heavy leather sandals.

What weapons did they use?

Legionaries were armed with a dagger, a short sword and a long spear. They had a shield to defend themselves.

Why was the army important to the Romans?

The first Roman army was put together to defend Rome. It was made up of ordinary citizens. All men between the ages of 17 and 60 could be called up to serve in the army. As Rome became more powerful and started to build up an empire, however, it needed a strong army which could conquer other countries and keep them under Roman control. Changes were made to the army. Instead of men being forced to become soldiers, volunteers were called for. The volunteers were well paid, well trained and well organised. As well as marching and fighting, these soldiers could build roads and bridges.

How long did soldiers serve?

Volunteer soldiers had to serve full-time in the army for 20 years. During this time they were well paid. When they retired they were given land or money to help them start a new life.

Why was the army so successful?

The Roman army was successful because its soldiers were well trained and orders were clearly given. Everybody knew what they had to do in a battle. It was also successful because supplies of food, drink and weapons were well organised and so the soldiers rarely went hungry or thirsty for long.

What were Roman forts like?

Roman forts were usually oblong in shape, surrounded by a high wall. There was a gate in the middle of each side and the roads which ran through these crossed in the centre and divided the fort into **four** main sections. Within each section were the barracks for the soldiers, the headquarters for the officers, stables for the horses, grain stores, baths, lavatories and a hospital.

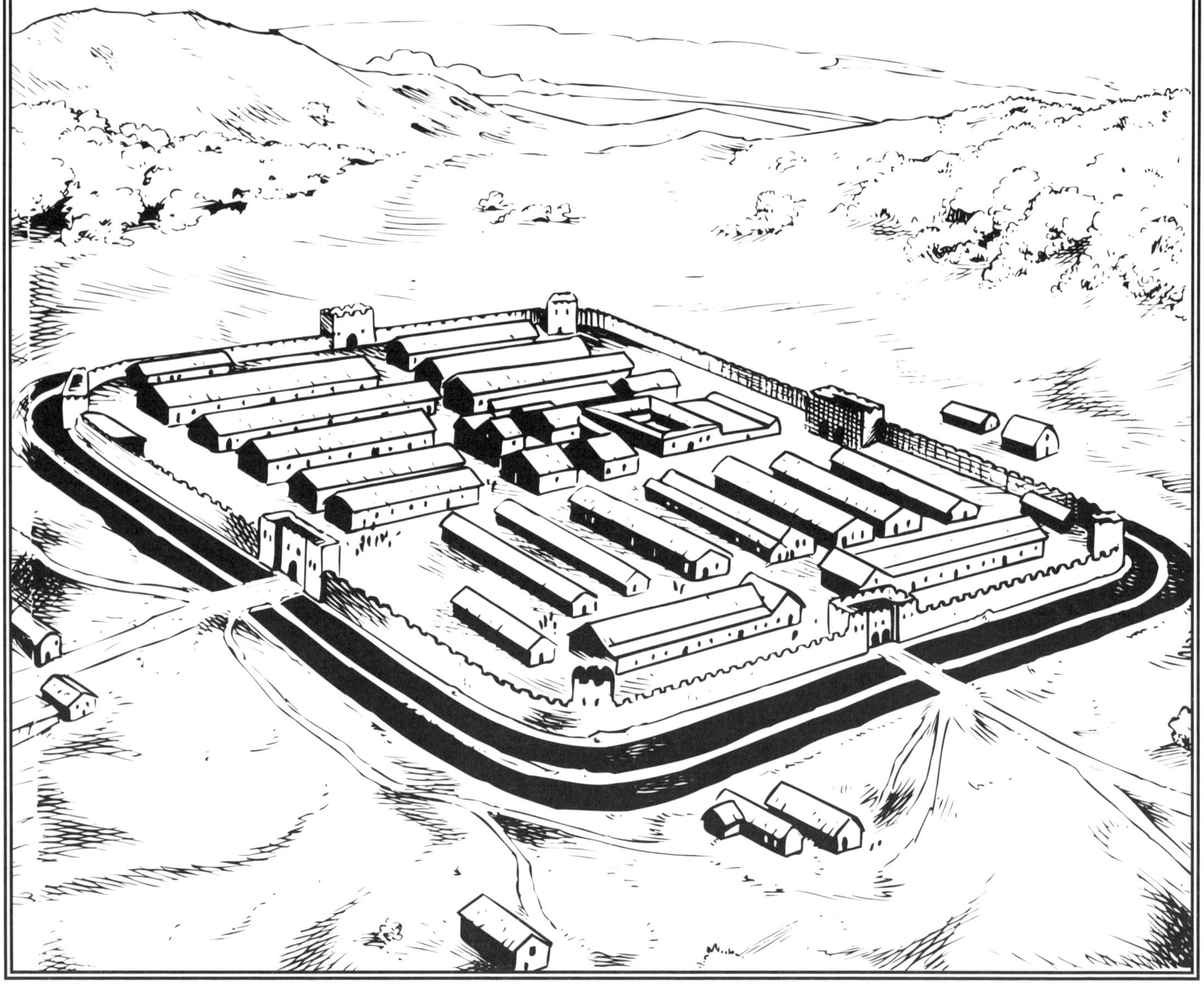

THE END OF THE ROMANS

17

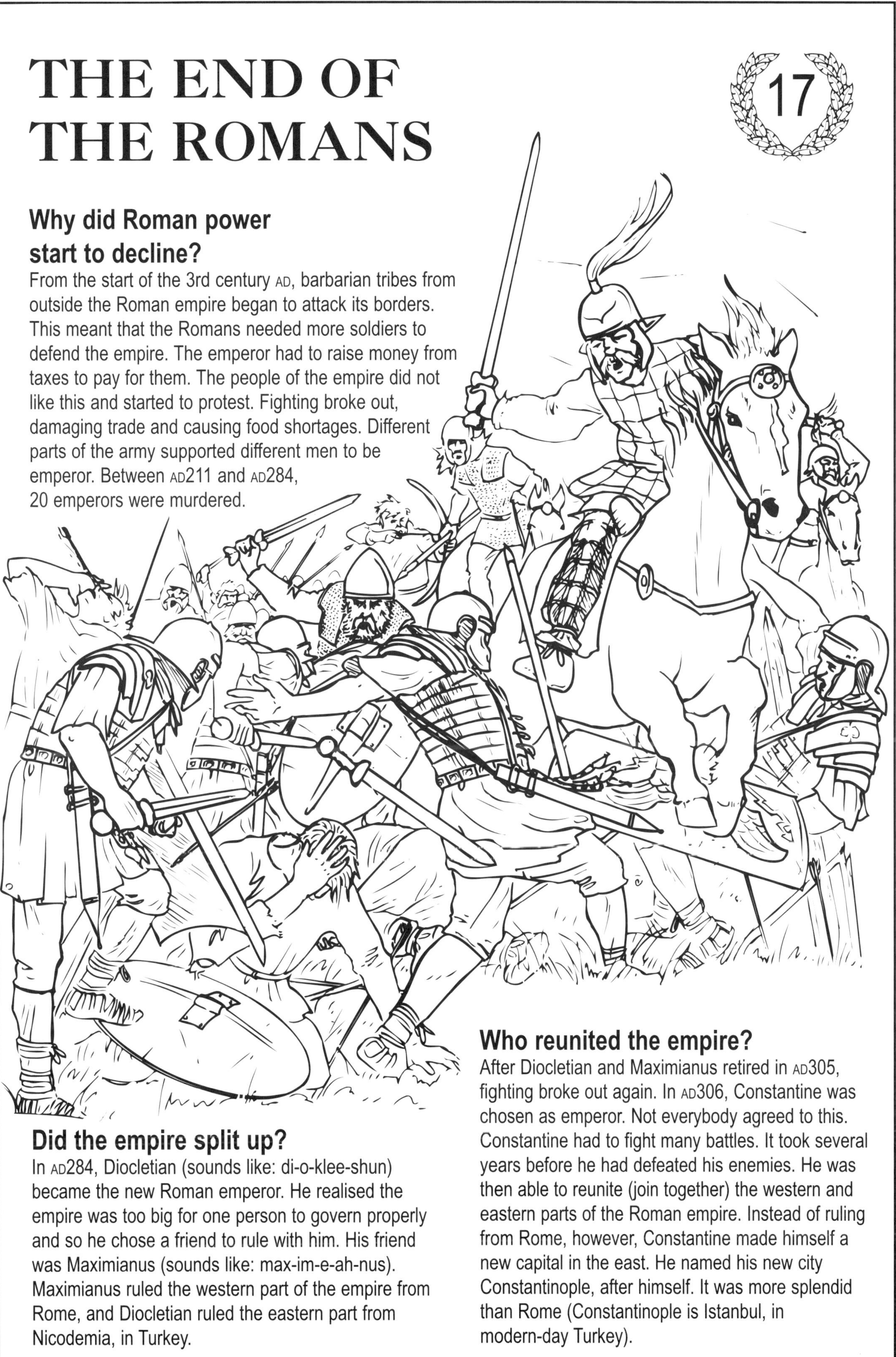

Why did Roman power start to decline?

From the start of the 3rd century AD, barbarian tribes from outside the Roman empire began to attack its borders. This meant that the Romans needed more soldiers to defend the empire. The emperor had to raise money from taxes to pay for them. The people of the empire did not like this and started to protest. Fighting broke out, damaging trade and causing food shortages. Different parts of the army supported different men to be emperor. Between AD211 and AD284, 20 emperors were murdered.

Did the empire split up?

In AD284, Diocletian (sounds like: di-o-klee-shun) became the new Roman emperor. He realised the empire was too big for one person to govern properly and so he chose a friend to rule with him. His friend was Maximianus (sounds like: max-im-e-ah-nus). Maximianus ruled the western part of the empire from Rome, and Diocletian ruled the eastern part from Nicodemia, in Turkey.

Who reunited the empire?

After Diocletian and Maximianus retired in AD305, fighting broke out again. In AD306, Constantine was chosen as emperor. Not everybody agreed to this. Constantine had to fight many battles. It took several years before he had defeated his enemies. He was then able to reunite (join together) the western and eastern parts of the Roman empire. Instead of ruling from Rome, however, Constantine made himself a new capital in the east. He named his new city Constantinople, after himself. It was more splendid than Rome (Constantinople is Istanbul, in modern-day Turkey).

Was the Roman empire invaded?

Around AD370, barbarian tribes from central Europe were attacked by people called the Huns. The Huns came from Asia. To escape these attacks, the barbarian tribes moved out of their homelands and into the Roman empire. This was the start of many invasions as people moved across Europe looking for safe places to live.

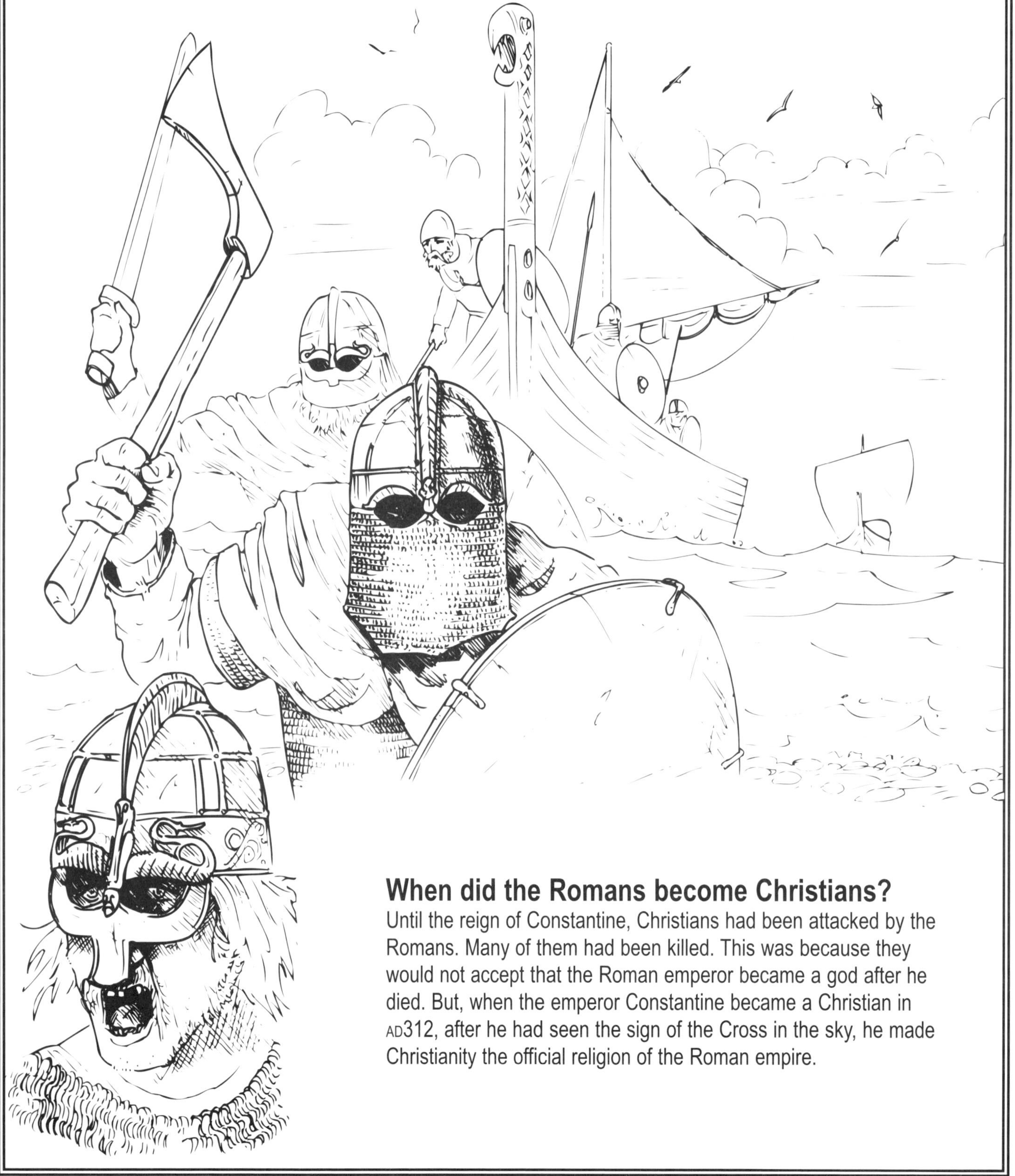

When did the Romans become Christians?

Until the reign of Constantine, Christians had been attacked by the Romans. Many of them had been killed. This was because they would not accept that the Roman emperor became a god after he died. But, when the emperor Constantine became a Christian in AD312, after he had seen the sign of the Cross in the sky, he made Christianity the official religion of the Roman empire.

WORDS TO DO WITH THE ROMANS

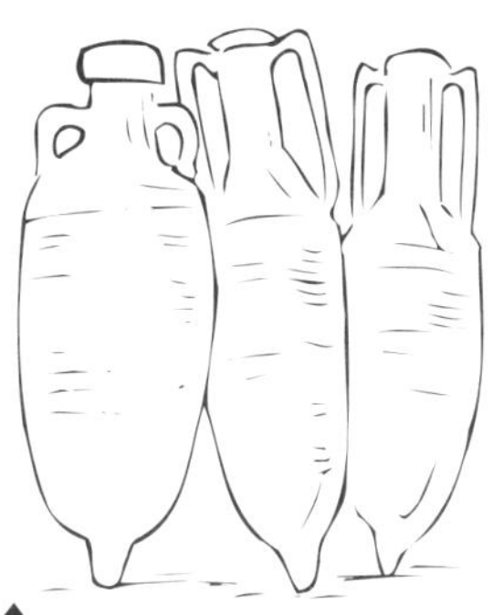

Aqueduct A bridge-like structure which carried water across valleys and into a town. Roman towns needed a good water supply.

Amphora A large pottery container which was used for storing and transporting wine, oil and other liquids.

Ballista A very powerful catapult made from strong timbers.
It used a tightly twisted rope which, when released, hurled stones and iron-tipped bolts over long distances.

Hypocaust
A system of warming the homes of the wealthy.
Hot air from a furnace circulated under the floor and warmed the room above.

Catacomb An underground cemetery made up of narrow passages with slots cut into the walls for burials. They were used by Christians before Christianity became the official religion of the Roman empire.

Stola A loose-fitting, ankle-length dress worn by married women. The stola could be made from wool, linen or silk and dyed red, yellow, green, blue, black, white or purple.

Mosaic
A picture usually made from little pieces of different coloured stone stuck on to a flat surface. Many were used to decorate floors, but some were also stuck on walls.

Toga A semi-circular piece of cloth, almost six metres long, which Roman men wore over their tunics when going out. It was pure white and usually made from wool. They draped it over their left shoulder, across the back and under their right arm, then across the chest and over the left shoulder again.

CREATE A MOSAIC

SHIELD	-	red and yellow
SWORD	-	black and grey
FACE	-	pink and red
LAUREL (ON SHIELD)	-	yellow and orange
HELMET	-	grey and white
CLOTHES	-	red and white

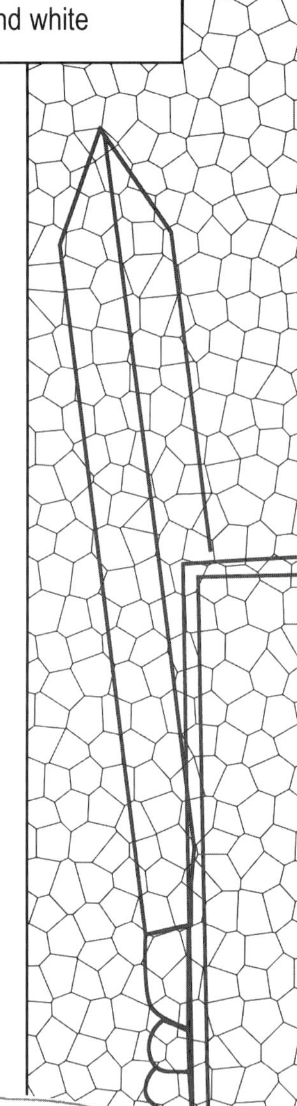

Colour each piece in the correct colour to complete this Roman mosaic.

30 ROMAN BRAIN BEATERS

1. **Which of these were Roman tribes?**

   a. Etruscans and Vikings
   b. Latins and Etruscans
   c. Latins and Remiums

2. **Who was the first legendary ruler of Rome?**

   a. Remus
   b. Romulus
   c. Numitor

3. **Who was the first Roman emperor?**

   a. Hadrian
   b. Trajan
   c. Augustus

4. **Which emperor conquered Dacia?**

   a. Trajan
   b. Constantine
   c. Augustus

5. **Who hid his bald head under a wig?**

   a. Nero
   b. Julius Caesar
   c. Constantine

6. **What name was given to a group of men, chosen in an election, to rule Rome?**

   a. rulers
   b. dictators
   c. senators

7. How did Julius Caesar die?

a. he was stabbed to death
b. he died from old age
c. he was killed by a chariot

8. What was the wealthy ruling class called in Rome?

a. physicians
b. patricians
c. prebitions

9. Who defeated the Romans at the battle of Allia?

a. Celts
b. Vikings
c. French

10. In which building did gladiators fight wild animals?

a. Pantheon
b. Forum
c. Colosseum

11. Why would people go to the Pantheon?

a. to watch chariot racing
b. to worship gods
c. to go shopping

12. Who had a column named after him, which celebrated his military victories?

a. Romulus
b. Julius Caesar
c. Trajan

13. In which English town did 11 kings surrender to the emperor Claudius?

a. Colchester
b. Kent
c. London

14. How did the Romans build roads in Britain?

a. as straight as possible
b. with lots of bends
c. over as many hills as possible

15. Why was Hadrian's Wall built?

a. to show off the Roman's building skills
b. to mark the boundary of the Roman Empire
c. to stop sheep from crossing it

16. Why do we think the Romans might have been to Ireland?

a. because Roman objects have been dug up there
b. because some Irish people look like Romans
c. because Irish people can speak Latin

17. Where did the Romans eat their meals?

a. sitting in tall chairs
b. lying on couches, from a low table
c. standing up, from servant's trays

18. Which drink was thought to benefit ill people?

a. milk
b. wine
c. water

19. Where were 11 year old boys educated?

a. grammarian
b. grammar school
c. grammaticus

20. Who was the god of wine?

a. Bacchus
b. Juno
c. Mercury

21. Who was the messenger of the gods?

a. Mars
b. Mercury
c. Neptune

22. Who was the god of the sea and fresh water springs?

a. Neptune
b. Juno
c. Jupiter

23. Who was the god of fire?

a. Vesta
b. Vulcan
c. Venus

24. Who was the head of each century in the Roman army?

a. emperor
b. legionaire
c. centurion

25. What did the 'standard bearer' carry?

a. a long pole with a dragon on top
b. a long pole with an animal skin on top
c. a long pole with a silver eagle on top

26. What weapons did legionaires use?

a. a dagger, a short sword and a long spear
b. an axe, a gun and a dagger
c. a knife, a spear and a pistol

27. Why was the Roman army so successful?

a. because its soldiers bullied its enemies
b. because its soldiers bribed its enemies
c. because its soldiers were well trained

28. How many sections were in a Roman fort?

a. 6
b. 4
c. 10

29. Why did the Roman empire start to decline?

a. too many Romans had been killed
b. the barbarian tribes started to attack its borders
c. Roman soldiers were too tired

30. What was a ballista?

a. a drink
b. a catapult
c. a sword

30 ROMAN BRAIN BEATERS

1. b	**6.** c	**11.** b	**16.** a	**21.** b	**26.** a
2. b	**7.** a	**12.** c	**17.** b	**22.** a	**27.** c
3. c	**8.** b	**13.** a	**18.** a	**23.** b	**28.** b
4. a	**9.** a	**14.** a	**19.** c	**24.** c	**29.** b
5. b	**10.** c	**15.** b	**20.** a	**25.** c	**30.** b

JULIUS CAESAR'S VERDICT

SCORE BETWEEN

0-5

You bring shame on the power of Rome!
You are only fit to be a Roman slave.

6-10

You'd better worship Minerva and learn something from the goddess of wisdom.

11-15

Must try harder!
Recite more Latin and Greek.

16-20

Good try!
A centurion would be proud of you.

21-25

Great score!
Caesar lets you be a standard bearer.

26-30

You are a great asset to the Roman empire.
Full of Roman wisdom!

WORD SEARCH

B	L	Q	B	R	L	Z	B	M	O	C	A	T	A	C
C	A	Y	F	Y	O	M	E	U	L	S	J	O	R	W
O	D	L	Q	E	C	M	F	B	X	E	U	Y	L	A
L	G	E	L	R	M	I	U	J	T	I	L	U	B	G
O	A	N	D	I	D	V	X	L	T	V	I	S	J	Q
S	J	G	W	P	S	R	P	C	U	K	U	F	A	K
S	N	P	K	M	G	T	S	I	T	S	S	M	H	C
E	A	C	H	E	O	U	A	A	C	R	C	B	V	S
U	L	O	R	G	M	H	D	S	U	N	A	P	J	U
M	O	E	A	E	Y	K	W	O	D	T	E	T	C	A
F	T	S	R	O	R	E	P	M	E	H	S	P	Q	H
Q	S	B	H	Z	C	N	X	I	U	U	A	W	K	O
X	D	P	Z	V	R	T	J	A	Q	Z	R	L	N	P
O	F	C	A	M	P	H	O	R	A	U	O	G	I	E
M	E	O	I	R	O	M	A	N	S	S	M	A	S	H

AMPHORA
AQUEDUCT
BALLISTA
CATACOMB
COLOSSEUM
EMPEROR
EMPIRE
JULIUS CAESAR
MOSAIC
REMUS
ROMANS
ROMULUS
STOLA
TOGA

ROMAN BOARD GAME

It's going to be a long journey – Rome wasn't built in a day!

INSTRUCTIONS

Tape this half of the board game to the other half on page 29.

You will need:
counters and a dice

You are Roman soldiers and are about to help build the Roman empire.

Using a counter for each player, roll the dice and move the number of spaces shown on the dice.

Follow the instructions on the spaces and the first player to reach FINISH is the winner!

You are a true defender of Rome. The Roman empire is now complete.

ANSWERS

Unscramble the gods p.14

Neptune

Diana

Jupiter

Venus

Saturn

Word search p.29

B	L	Q	B	R	L	Z	B	M	O	C	A	T	A	C
C	A	Y	F	Y	O	M	E	U	L	S	J	O	R	W
O	D	L	Q	E	C	M	F	B	X	E	U	Y	L	A
L	G	E	L	R	M	I	U	J	T	I	L	U	B	G
O	A	N	D	I	D	V	X	L	T	V	I	S	J	Q
S	J	G	W	P	S	R	P	C	U	K	U	F	A	K
S	N	P	K	M	G	T	S	I	T	S	S	M	H	C
E	A	C	H	E	O	U	A	A	C	R	C	B	V	S
U	L	O	R	G	M	H	D	S	U	N	A	P	J	U
M	O	E	A	E	Y	K	W	O	D	T	E	T	C	A
F	T	S	R	O	R	E	P	M	E	H	S	P	Q	H
Q	S	B	H	Z	C	N	X	I	U	U	A	W	K	O
X	D	P	Z	V	R	T	J	A	Q	Z	R	L	N	P
O	F	C	A	M	P	H	O	R	A	U	O	G	I	E
M	E	O	I	R	O	M	A	N	S	S	M	A	S	H

This pack has been approved by the YAC: Young Archaeologists' Club, Bowes Morrel House, 111 Walmgate, York, YO1 9WA